In the Flight of Stars

In the Flight of Stars

Dorothy Roberts

GOOSE LANE

Published with the assistance of the Canada Council and the New Brunswick Department of Tourism, Recreation & Heritage, 1991.

Some of these poems have been previously published in *Antigonish Review, The Cormorant, The Fiddlehead, Hudson Review, Journal of General Education*, League of Canadian Poets Newsletter, *Pivot, The Proceedings of the Charles G.D. Roberts Symposium* (Sackville: Mount Allison University, 1984), *The Self of Loss* (Fredericton: Fiddlehead Poetry Books, 1976) and *Sonora Review*.

Cover painting: "Etheric Form," by James W.G. (Jock) Macdonald, 1935, oil on panel, 31 cm x 38 cm, courtesy Barbara Macdonald, from the collection of Max Merkur.
Book design by Julie Scriver.
Printed in Canada by Ronalds Printing.
Bound in Canada by Martin Bookbinding.

Canadian Cataloguing in Publication Data

Roberts, Dorothy, 1906 -
  In the flight of stars

Poems.
ISBN 0-86492-097-0

I. Title.

PS8535.O23I6 1991   C811'.54   C91-097560-4
PR9199.2.R62I6 1991

Goose Lane Editions
248 Brunswick Street
Fredericton, New Brunswick
Canada E3B 1G9

Contents

A Vertical Figure

Passing On Spoons

Return by Petitcodiac

River Valley Expanse

A Vertical Figure

The Sun

Coming down the stairs   meeting sun-patches
hitherto somewhere else   the day advances
to go back to when they were just so   is a whole year's expanse
and ignores the clock on the shelf

The day glows solid   beyond the walls and patches
the carpets and the floorboards in reminiscence
of last year's equivalent season
dated only on an earlier calendar

The day shifts onward   its ritual hours
welcoming the sun in a sequence of windows
like a ghost story being planted   the whole circumstance
time as we capture it   whatever happens in the meters

We are asking what is transformed
by this structure   the problem remains
and if bevelled the older mirrors
send out a decoration of rainbows

The Sunbeam

A sunbeam coming to earth
    seeking out a suitable place
where sun might be at work
affable with distance   the perfect found
prints shadows of bedposts   chairs and desk
                    reclines

this is the advent
    of a true harmony   when the hand
clasps the condolence:

Yes, your shadow shall be imprinted
    here at the hour
I pass   pulse in
and transform the narrow to the supreme

radiance greater than the glow   I stream
widely   because the concentrated human
              in its small cubicle
comes here to pass away

A history is nowhere seen but how it stays

You know that actually I'm given to flowers
and the green leaf producing all the hours

and that history folds in its own book and withers
along with what it destroys?

                          "Yes"

and yet you expect a blessing?   Sunshine rests

To the Sun in Age

How good will you be to what courts you still   asks your
   pardon
for absence of more graces   asks your instruction
for loving still the light hours   asks your forgiveness
for not providing the maximum of life where you lower
   yourself
asks your understanding:

that I stay   more than a branch
more than fruit, more than a petal even   more than pollen
or is it pollen that I hope to be besides another moment
so accepting the light that it looks good on the thinned skin
of such being   and the exposed vein   running its course

Sitting in the sun
seeing change more stressfully than in any other way
seeing the skin and the vein
drenched in sunlight like the flesh of — flash
a dive into the river of light
of long-ago islands or pregnancies
mounding the earth   from those years back

Now I no longer feel anything owed me   and the light is
   benign
that allows the moments to stay
aslant on the withering skin   intense

The sun is everywhere and at any age
or stage of life it may be intimately had
and at this time
lights the contortions of the veins
running under the skin   but in their stress

seeming to have the ways that conceive
of being like the mind   a leaf
Responsible as a leaf I compose something

Late Hours

                                     two on a bench
sit bundled up   towards evening light
path winding away where other people have left

Silence is different on a bench   really speech
communication and peace   and the unloading

yes, a boat, not quite beached, is the image
for the bench   and though the tenants haven't left
some weight is gone   and they sit and float
in the crystal clear darkening dusk

What of it?   much   they are not afraid
not to be in Time   to be left out
It means they don't partake
of supper and the enclosures in the night

Instead they drain
the declining light
the park time and the sun and even the autumn runs out
    for them
still they remain   they float after an explanation

Imprint: In Praise of Time

An old head on the pillow persists in dreams
not dreams now   waking   they are images
the very ones that came when life was thus

a nuggety package now   for no one else
holds this same vision   and many much in doubt
about this time   want it   or rather just
the knowledge claimed from the derivatives

knowledge not come of this authentic spring
this source of image quietly harbouring
the very people clustered   round the table
or all upset in waves of argument   what should be done
   next?

the people of that vision   dining so properly
till manners break   and in the ensuing uproar
   a time is gone   another takes its place
another and another come to pass

oh head upon the pillow   ancient head even
white hair now streaming
   none may now know what you know   images
blazing the perpendicular of the skies
so long within their gleam   more and more in distance

Old head lie on the pillow with your load
loadstone of all that   family lore that lures
inquirers to demand a proof of theme
give none   die out behind the fading eyesight
the eyes that shine

the years pile on   and what you see as truth
dims out abroad   only in your eyes glimmers

You see the past assembled as it has been
there in its time   before a change of tone
took it away to where all views are wrong
but for this single image   inner sight
set up within a mind of aged ferment

Old head upon the pillow   can you forsake
the world enough to hold your vision intact
kept there as truth   a nugget in a bone
constant   although the stuff of which the brain
is made is wedded to all realms of thought

A Marvel

One of the images in my brain
is a galaxy seen through a telescope years ago
at a distance from where my life is now,
small light blur becoming only in thought one of the great
    views

One of the views that can be looked at from another time
so distance lays out a plan   full of light   full of expansion
expanded back into itself and condensed
into one of the great grounds of sense

Only in thought is it realized
as more than a white breath   an enterprise in itself
where further laws are likely to be the same laws
to hold poised the great exuberance

And on and on to convert its size
into an intensity as immense   an action as intense
and governable in ways as ours
or how does it follow the heavens and yet can be recalled
to the telescope again even at this hour?

By time   years ago it was first seen
it has settled itself into the laws of dream
for the laws are the same
for inventing the telescope's eye as being in the brain
they light and relight   in inexhaustible profusion the
    sources of energy
a note of profoundest proportion earns them the name

More and more goes on and surrounds
the eclipsed self as the galaxy proves
in one of the great views   given of light
on the vast horizon of being
on the outskirts of all we don't have   do have and marvel at

The Black Walnut

The image of that bare tree
insists itself upon everyday

it has dropped at last its ill-advised nuts
too many and still undeveloped

they lie strewn

it has lost its leaves at the same time
            presents itself   in the early morning
slowly as light

outlines the array of branches
in blue growing transparent
against the window glass

form of forgetfulness
the struggle with nuts
a folly dropping also many twigs

till to the eyes that see it
            time's lingering image
branches arranged by thought

The Clothes

Out in the early morning   I met the sun
full glare on my clothesline
dazzling me out of countenance while I hung
the long row in the stillness   but for the birds

They made a clamour   translating light to sound
and the clothes did not flap   this sunrise   nor dangle limp
but were alive   with air mixed in with light

and lived more powerfully than for my present flesh

The birds and the light spread   the day
extricated itself   from this profound departure
from humankind   as all the laundry got ready
                              to sunbathe bravely

(unlike myself preferring day to night)

spreading and introducing itself
                   to neighbours who raise shades:

Who is that neighbour new to us   gone back into her house
after her wash is hung   to every bit of sun
taking advantage of us who sleep in later?

an old person no doubt: so early abroad
means up at night   and the clothes hanging
introduce her estate   to this old neighbourhood
                              raising its shades to light

A Vertical Figure

Plum emergence is the start   of light in the east spreading
until radiance   that shall never be matched all day reaches
across roofs and trees seen from other windows

This is what we have from our star
such a one as twinkles somewhere   and here
sets up the tree in place . . . but to go back into the night

so as to know Age   a vertical figure up
from rest   caught into mirrors   at the window to peer out

and down the stairs   the front door locked   and passing it
                                        for the tea and books

with the tea to lurch   above cellar stairs   yes
by mistake thinking this
                    the door to the hallway   steadied at a step
the first having been down   placed   already hung in space
                    the cup of tea flying — what grace
saving the situation   and going back to think in the kitchen

think   think   how bones survive   and how one wishes
them wholeness throughout life   and life continuing
into some sky of being   (the fragments to be picked up
the coming day — a cup slopping tea splintered)

a toast to be drunk now   freshly in the kitchen
then the veined hands   thin-skinned
move along a shelf of books in the sitting room

a light to sort them by   and the desire to disperse
one's own lot into others and the reverse
                              Oh phantoms they are not

or at the window half the moon gone out

Glimmers of Age

I see the glimmer of intelligence
open at dawn and seek a perspective

last stars are one to it   in this aged eyesight
                                    and the light

comes dressing the trees
in their falling leaves

not much not much a touch of all abroad
this comes to the window closest
breathes on its glass

by light itself filling the tree branch
from the days of Chinese willows and poets
under them I begin by this light to fill the day

by the first blue light   the dawn in the stream of sequence

the Chinese knew how to advance
to the last step of art off into space
from the cliff edge   from the branch   poor eyesight
tracing the mysterious curve of despair
so that it seems elate

The Shack

When travelling I kept seeing an occasional
shack   on the mountainside   clinging

When travelling I would see it   and go by
with it still in my thoughts no matter what next
and my sorrow for it somehow clinging and remembered

It was the shell   for a form of life   I apprehended
when travel is done and the language of life
and the beat of the landscape   give back the self

                              and passing by
I thought of shells each the same   and different

That was when I travelled   and now here
in the mountain hut   hear the wind go by
and the rain come so close that it is here
and the snow covers all

This is the hut of life   the tarred boards
echoing the rain   supporting the snow-cloud

giving themselves to a domain that has little other word
than the wind bringing down the leaves at the window

An echoing kind of place where I dwell now
remembering sometimes any passing sorrow

Timing by Ocean

A statement of seaworth   proven of old for good
comes in these books on the shelves

            The sea has shrunk
it's shrunk under the flights
joining continent to continent overnight
but mostly in the fringes contaminated

Thus every memento is a plus

and all the mementos add up
by telling of ocean how it existed
in History at least and how it can still

even though ages move by   each with its period
            and that for which Ada lived left the bric-a-brac

on shelves   and in the trunk: ticket stubs
cabin lists   menus   program of the concert
in which she sang   mid-ocean   for the Sailors' Orphan Fund

left too perhaps the plumes of smoke
that trailed a week across to Europe
as some of the red still in ocean sunsets

Sea-time must absorb that

on its way back and back
as waves turn round in mid-ocean with the wind

back to the time a sea-going ballad
made history of the spirits of the drowned

three sturdy sons allowed at the home hearth
until they were beckoned back to the light on waves

and Saxons who rode like chargers the crests
to pillage the coastal settlements

lost in the storms their star of guidance
         recurrent at the masthead through many travels
broke into Poetry beyond themselves   here bound

The mariner (ancient later) who slew the albatross
and was   with his companions   curst
in drought becalmed in blazing light
that showed the creatures he must love in depth
until he did   then heaven above
moved waters and wind   and he came home to tell the tale
     of it

Listen   the sea-roar here on Dover Beach
tells the old tale of pebbles grating ceaselessly
cleansed thoroughly and letting time begin
again as it might be

Passing On Spoons

Lamp of Life

Inside the chimney a wick carries a small light
absorbed from the oil base   that's good
Don't let it tip   don't let its light spread
to the orange and red walls   to the bay windows
to the door with its glimmering panes of coloured glass
overhead   to the turrets and the stairs
to the hanging curtains and those looped back

to the uncertainties in every closet
to the commanding views   and the hope of reprisals
for every curse and lament   to the stone entry steps
to the hearth and the beds   where sleep left time
                                    unrecorded

A Place

There were no elders   to control our actions
what we did and we clamoured and in all innocence
knew nothing of place where it meets with happenings

only the broken lock   iron fisted falling helplessly
from the oaken door and the darkness welling out
with the sound of the nearby waterfall

There were no elders in control   just as now
when I move around alone and explore
possibilities for the distribution of what I have now

There are no elders to control
what leaves a house empty after what has been here
More and more, children, the place becomes uninhabitable

The shingled outer walls, the sunshine
at a small distance the noisy waterfall
A house stands empty   autumn controls it like a tree

Lament: the Self that Sleeps

Mice are the animals that I know best
in a paroxysm of soiling as they wrench
or paralyzed   peering up to see the tormentor

London — wartime — rooming house   mice remembered
    most
in the crowd captured by the constant access
to something somewhere: old woman's crumbs
child's bits here and there   and always the bait

so many traps that I unset   This is the excursion
to when I lived more than all else these small gray persons
dying and tormented in the ancient basements

Greatest of my first loves
I flew to their rescue with my fists and tears
Is this I protecting my old age
who once sprang traps, chased cats, fought boys, tricked
    landladies?

My first love squeals in the trap — not dead
myself that sleeps encounters the whole episode
even as it wakes   the sound   the snap
the billion deaths   don't lessen one that struggles

Myself that sleeps lies listening to the sounds
my acts have ordered   May God comfort
these that he made for undoing   by great numbers
each with this death in store   the trespassers

In rooming houses   bleak in the London suburbs
I rescued them from every form of death

They were the only survivors
of my impassioned judgments   innocent
in the closets and corners

The mouse grows ever larger with its resistance
I am inadequate now to the measure of life
I live my lack   the mouse lives in the trap
won't die as I wish   I ask for help

My aged self lies trapped within its sleeping
its deeds lie all around as does its property
Sleep mouse please sleep the deepest sleep of all
and wake no more to be a mouse at all

A Home on Needham Street

Three attic bedrooms under the peaked roof
of one of the narrow houses on Needham Street

fixed now for the three of us, brother and sisters

and below the middle floor   occupied by the house owner
our parents on the ground floor: bedroom   kitchen
    sitting-room

Was this a comedown for them after the years of travel?

But the life that was beginning to form
in us more definitely went on
in the three bedrooms of the attic   for the first time

so exclusively   definitely given room

                        Goodridge to his drawing
turns again on waking   leaves the grotesques of dreams
rampant on each flyleaf   of books brought up in a heap
to his room overlooking the street

I concentrate on Keats
coming from the poems to the letters
answer him with more promises

pledge from this acquired distance
all my life's years and love and sacrifice
to bring about a difference in his   no death

Who has done this with hope in time past?

Teddy looks into her mirror
                    in a room I don't share
shed with light from her one window
high above the old back garden

Childish retention of being the youngest
vanishes in the mirror's depth
where the new score takes place
no wonder she looks and looks

So our parents on the ground floor had become roots

and in between was the old house of stairs
and a middle floor where the aged owner stayed

and over the ceilings that sloped to our attitudes
the peaked roof long ago raised for a climate of snows

An Early Interior

The picture could stop a passionate tide of feeling
from taking hold   it was a wedge, a stopper
a filter between an overpowering world
and this one with its own design   it quietly
stopped the place from really being here

let it in formally   a front door
propriety   without it the uproar
is terrible   they cry they still are there

A set of people had that house
at their disposal once
rooms stressed by doors
gave voices a chance
to stay and be heard   quarrels were enhanced

My sister was all vibrations then
(many young men were on her track)
who died at length four thousand miles hence
she sparkled like a sun and moon together
still could years later
but she was then all charm, the sunnier daughter
My brother drew the picture

My brother made the picture, sitting absorbed
in all its directions   leading to a vision
he hoped was coming, abstracted as he poised there
practising his outstanding future

What was I doing?   I was breaking
the jagged edge of the lost land, leaving

"I look for structure," he said
making lines that bisected
a corner   enclosed a door wide
made an exit into the entrance hall

Why was my mother bitter, only forty-nine then
but carrying destruction in her vehemence
"Don't you like being a mother?"   "No," she said

"I go by light," he said
right to the floor   angles and surfaces rousing the eye
and colours: he had only tempera   to lavish on enough
Chips came away before I got the glass
behind which the picture stayed for years and years
and years   giving perspective

He painted   Mother's vehemence kept intact
rooms we were trying to leave   from which he painted
all that would move him most
                          stroke on stroke to greatness
of other views
                          while the effervescent sister
could only move in more and more tormented grooves

around him the doors opened and closed and his lines
    revealed
something of what went on though he wasn't listening

My sister moved into more that would never be saved
and tried to break it all with tears and cries

She never gave up her glow

My father in another room was typing on his story
and wreathed in smoke the words came out and added to
  his lifetime

They left the home, they left the doors
the rooms were but a shadow
My brother had stayed to line the shape
of one room to another
and from this structure surged the lines
he followed to his deathbed

Daphne lived there with her golden hair
her step as light as a feather
her tears and her sobs and her sparkling eyes
her troubles that bubbled over
And Mother was full of bitterness
as she busied herself with moving

Part of the culture of my home
the picture held at bay
the stormy side of promise
kept my pact with that time

It stays outlined upon the wall
from which descendants move it

Women and Light

Women of Vermeer   have fulfilment
only in what he says of them   benign
sun   secluding their work from the forces of destruction
benign sun   outlining what has to be done
and the whole tapestry of brick, cloth, skin

He gives them work that is never done
gold weighing and lace to make and milk to pour
and scrub and rub and the calm light pours
time away   over their intent forms
Brush strokes are absorbed
into the surfaces by the consistent splendour

No Story

What is so wonderful about pieces of art
is that they blossom so late in other hearts
and unfortellable places and times apart
from any particular trend

I have three children of ancestors on a bright auspicious
    morning
ranged in one big chair for a painting of decorum

Photographs tell tales   but these children buried
in deepest long ago   their lives fulfilled
somewhere or lost   give me this morning's glow

no mother or nurse dressed them with more care
than I in this sunbeam look on their aspects fair
soft shadow of desolation?   but there is none

and paint's delayed appreciation of volumes
keeps just one carefully open morning

as here in me the volume of reception
is at its height   the while the day begins   and the night
sinks into nothingness in the light

        Into the ever-recurring combination:
children and art   comes my life

No voices have they to tell their beginning
or how it ends in the days departed long ago

instead with their eyes they sing

and the frilled girl between two dominant brothers
shows for a moment history's thrust
how much sorrow then came to women

But this is in the morning
        here brought forward
in the placement of the three children
in the preferences of light to show them

Two

women walking in the rain
to a cottage they share on the moor
in the north   they're nearly there

What awaits them?   just their fear
their closeness   their goodness
each room   the stair
just the windows widening the view of rain over the moor

just the way   sitting together   they look out at the weather

                              Who are they missing
as they come near   who are they missing as they talk and
   hear?

What is the rain?
is it what searched out the crack in the roof
and touches the night with its reiteration:

who do they miss   other than each other
where did they come from walking together
the groceries   the library   the graveyard
the railway track   the busline   They're here

back where they were   worn with their own identities
                        they keep up
strenuous adhesions to the just

Losses in Blue

One being the loss of my sister   I catch on blue
the colour of her eyes   as belonging to me
search for it all over the place

and take it personally
in edges of fields and woodlands
in flower star and bell

in blue vetch   bluebells   blue flags   blue-eyed grass
in water divided by cloud forms from the blue above
in the small opening of forget-me-nots
in the deeps of sky blue amongst clouds

in shadows of a snowy winter such as we knew
shifting on glaze under a cloudless day

especially now in the very early morning
deep through the near bough and held till faded

She went out to California and wore dark glasses
against the singeing of the sun to which she was sensitive
That was long ago   and her eyes have closed since

nothing closes like blue about the woods and fields
in morning glory on the vine
in flower star and bell

Passing on Spoons

There's no way of holding them makes them more
than the dessert size spoons they are

    "Why then do you think of them as valuable?"

They're beautiful   I inherited them   I pass them on

    "Oh   family pieces   they're valuable to you"

to others too   I claim
because of their age   their perfection
spoons with the flow of line
reserved for perfection   and hallmarks deep-cut still

    "They must be a blessing"   they are

through poverty and stress distinguished
by their attributes of then   nothing touching them
in their tissue in a drawer
or on the table   other than our hands and food
in unison   they are not knives or forks

just precious spoons

and now as I pass them on they will not change
they are not cast to do so   they will stay

just as they were — but for thinness — when made
where silverware took shape
in Queen Anne's reign

having nothing to do with her pains

"Whom do you pass them on to — a museum perhaps
in our time of not honouring such family relics?"

or to one not in the strictest lineage
daughter   grandchild   as I was

Return by Petitcodiac

Petitcodiac Map

Helping myself out I observe a map
set in a cold land: roads cross it
as does a forest   border   as do steps
of inhabitants

as I observe   it seems the best
means of transposing   my older self

Who's going to count the crust-breaking tracks
that leave no mark upon the land
who's going to count where the wind went

who's going to draw the line   at sight
picking like stars the homely lights

that's the advantage of a map
childish marks where the sleds went
roads and the paths with Grandfather's steps
even to where the doors are locked

Here at the border in tangled trees
night cloaks   the crossing   and other paths
carry the hurry of rabbit and fox

or I may cross here   further south
where stolen and stretched the distances
don't count for much   lost in stars

The Homely Lights

What might this entrance call for next?
  women perhaps   lighting the nearby lights
that shining bring together the village
  scattered about the snow-glazed fields

the flames that poise in the chimneyed lamps
trained to control the evening haunts
and all the ways of this last stretch
of hours before the stars are most

The wicks are trimmed in the morning light
and chimneys cleaned of oily smoke
that might have flared there when a door was opened

stirring a skirt or shawl about

Women control this light sequestered
in its thin chimney   for the guidance
of many a step   they pass the windows
from room to room on the way to bed

window to window   they throw frost patterns
on outer night
                how far they reach
who can tell   but afterwards
shadows continue up the stairs

A Lamp Relit

What is the outcome of these lights
first coming into sight

under the heavenly ones   over the fields
verifying the houses?

They're faint   behind frost at the windows   shift sometimes
when a lamp is moved   as is the custom
though always indoors   these being a light
of the inner being   made by the pause

to light it   to carry it   thinking
                              dark enough now
earlier each day   or other thought
more applicable to a need

                    need by need   and the night need
sometimes as a call: a lamp relit

in the deep night's darkness
and over a pillowed head held   while shadows
faces   hands   together sought a cure-all
that often went little beyond what the light could do

this hurries the footsteps down the sloping field
and over the threshold   stamping in from the cold

Figures of Age

Separating themselves from the sleepers
in the chambers above
they arrive at the kitchen with their lamp

                    the fire is built up
crackling and heating the pipe to the upstairs
the kettle starts to tilt its lid
and against the dark   the frost covers the windows almost

Voices are only part of chores
dividing and uniting   his   hers
till the time for prayer arrives
          while their shadows repeat each act
and blend and separate

Conspiracy seems the key to this
by which they would inherit the earth
to be held always in this balance

Not at all   the prayer says:
Renunciation is the word   His   hers   his   hers

                    It would be against the Word
to go beyond time that is theirs
repeated   now to those above
wakening in the winter dark

The day will not whiten the window for a while yet

The Berries

The wintergreen berries uncovered
                    unsnowed, it is really
reveal themselves as red   bright and cheery
the apples of the birds to come

picked by children
while their frosty mittens   lie thrown to the side
with the snow they scraped

unsettling the seasons perhaps   but with wintry name
for the nippy supply of the clusters
bright on the tongue

this is just after Sunday school   the afternoon long-
shadowed at the edge of the wood

bring birds to these too

Zenith

A load of wood comes slowly
the little dappled mare with her red sleigh
travels   fast for the setting
but is seen quite awhile

Who is fortunate enough to own her
see that step from the position of the driver?
not a glamorous person   an old farmer   retired
having as his zenith   this flight   What better?

There she goes running   the perpetually white landscape
her foal-laden belly   hidden in time not ripe yet
her death when its time came   not yet in perspective
just the roads criss-crossing to set her off

just the bells ringing in profusion from the harness

End of a Day

Tough figures predominate out of doors
children blown by the wind into scarecrows
or standing mute in the cold evening till supper draws
them indoors   men grown   heavy with wood
brought in   out for more   while the light still holds

lamps within now   a woman passes
windows   lanterns for the outside
taken from nails   lit   the outhouse
sends out its cold gleam   dramatic

even the moon has no position   removed as this is
pathway beaten

Later, supper done, the rocker
settles itself even after
Grandmother's to bed   and daughters
pass the windows heavily frosted

Rocker

Rocking is so little   it only gains ascendancy
by going back to the trees in the forest

they rock too   and have within them
the same rings of promise
            of years to come as years accumulated

but these at home are cut on the bias   aslant and show
        a human attitude in design   and go
back and forth   slowly   bringing on the scene

things come and gone   the design is finished

            polished
persistent as that in the forest
                        creak

and the sons returning   from death in childhood
come into the scene   as Grandmother rocks
and the hours   hold the years wanted
                back   forth   onward

The trees sway in the forest and their rings
are the design from which the rocker repeats
its catechism   the catechism within it

The Caller

Grandfather knocked and got turned away
was it by the old woman herself
or by the wind?   that's what he asked himself
on the way back
promising return   for in his parish
all must be visited   and she was
there with the forest trees at the edge

There would be return   in any case
whether she or the wind   or the wind at her wish
cut off his words   though his bread was taken
in at the crack before the slam shut them

on opposite sides   and the wind within might even
be present at the lone bread cutting

come in by way of the chimney   or by the window flame
past the fluttering candle   or by the firewood
she brought in from wind-fallen about the forest

So he went down with his dominant step
even as he had climbed   and would
through the snow and its crust

and the forest at attention stood in the dusk

Sledding to Sunset

       with energy ignited like the stars
at ages eight to ten   or is it twelve
the kind that travels with the sun
       and breathes cold into flame

while on the snow the spread of light lasts
long as energy is in sight   bedazzling the glaze

with scarves   toques   mittens   red

Just for a little while to be the challenge
of sun's capacity   and back and forth
exchange excess   climbing again to course

the glittering hillside

       Scarcely above the treetops
the sun slants   downwards to icy crust
tangles before plunging
       leaves the red glow

is this enough   to close the simple story
                 east to west
or add it to the calendar for distance?

At the Church

They are just a coherent group of people
who usually come together to worship

who gather now to watch their structure
now burning into the snow

relics have been rescued
heat closes the door shape   windows blaze
steeple falls   and the beams
furred a moment fall too   flames rage
into the light of night   putting out effectively
all lights that surround or come from even as close
as the moon itself

This is very human   the white faces fade
in their scarves of mourning   turn to one another
as the flames sink   and the wind comes back cold again

The stars make a comeback   the moon returns
and the chars sink into their embers
Such are alone now

Let the lights blink out in the body of embers
and as the stars sink into the morning crimson
it is left to the forests to renew

River Valley Expanse

.

Years of the River: to T.G.R.

You didn't go without
what you had   in small poems
pure flights of sound
colour and situation   light touch and rapid water

A life-long pursuit   brought the river forever with you
verbally and with the liveliest prepositions
setting the whole landscape active   from boyhood to age
omitting only winter   the white sheet

In the midst of changing and threat of it and struggle
went the river a word order
of little poems treasured
scents and sounds   myths and adventures
Winter was omitted
but for the tremendous break-up

Then came the springtime   catkins spilling
into the water their pollen
logs on their way down to the broad river
mouth   birds from the south
canoes putting out

Summer was situated in the islands
had places there to be its full self
such blossoms, green ranks of reeds   water
creatures   blue arch of hours
almost at a standstill like the islands

You didn't go without
any of these times throughout your life
By way of prepositions   formality was established

in a small concourse
of autumn evening   flocks half in
transit and the water lapping
and the good of the beach fire about to happen

such a fragrant driftwood
brought to its arranged pile
whispers go on in several atmospheres
at once   and the day is ended

The Snowflakes

What seems a problem is   Ethel's demeanour which
takes expression from her staying with snow   drifts
when at the first flakes she wished to turn and go

but couldn't because of the way she was brought to Canada
by our parents' advance of pay   for passage by steamer

here from Jamaica
she was walking with the three of us
stopping only at curbs   till the first snowflakes
but passage still unearned   she stayed

Married upriver   and now her descendants
stay on in the recurrent snow drifts
while we are gone   long gone   and the nation takes

this change to its current self

Ethel who walked the Fredericton streets with us
stopping at curbs   and for the fall of flakes
that halted her   though so at home to us

Children in Depth

Oromocto river flats   relaxation of dress
(back home at last)   as flowers nod their living diadems

so flowers enhance   are native to   a countryside
dance   nod   and welcome children scarcely taller

The blue-eyed grass   is deeper in the daisies
and brown-eyed susan above   the harebells   buttercups
    and vetch

the morning glories of that tilt of hours
till noon   surprising children   to find these listless
past reprieve amongst their lavish foliage

we had a time with flowers and fireflies
and knew we were native too   where the river strews
shore edge with blocks of cedar from the mills
rolled all smooth waterwise and carrying us
beyond our depths   holding on in absolute trust
unknown abroad   even on the stoutest ships

Camouflage

A deceptive expedient was putting children aboard
  circumspection might then be assumed

and so through the ocean we ploughed

camouflaged to look like waves or clouds
harmonizing porpoises or vagrant islet

whatever   escaping the periscope's eye
into the on and on beneath the sky

and in the dark   of all personal light
every porthole blackened out

till terminal reached   (storied island
embargoed)   the real cause for travel

came out   and we in innocence went shoreward

O War of Opposites   as it is claimed
on all sides   seen and unseen   hidden and proclaimed

and waves going onward   the same   the same

A Vision of World War One

1 Stage

Can I do anything for World War One   pick out a plum
of meaning missed before in the event
from which the world has never steadied
now my lifetime of knowing it (absurd and resplendent,
layered over by nearly everything)
must sink with my going out of sight?

War came in like a character to the Folkestone stage
menacing, posturing, unafraid
And the stage seemed set out for it
unshaken even by the raids that split some houses, rubbled
   a street
stayed dramatically layered with channel beach
lower walk or Leas, chalk cliff and Upper Leas
hotels, avenues stretching off into the sheep-dotted downs
scene all laid out for its presence, not undone enough
to count its loss   a band playing the stepped-up march

Searchlights stretched over the sky and criss-crossed
then swept down over the English Channel
waves   searching and prying in dark upheaval for signs

Windows were covered black at night and sealed tight
not a ray to guide the enemy to our support
of the fighting and the sacrifice with all our might
planes hid in the dark of the lowering clouds
zeppelins coming out like silver cigars

What can a child's eye do to such a sight
but pick out its glimmering details from thought in later life
where those black-muffled windows crack sometimes?

2 Invaders

We were the first invaders of the land
come across the ocean to add to the crowd
caught here in Folkestone while our father served in France
and the World was readjusted beyond anyone's word
We were the addition at which the nation cheered and
   frowned

taking up part of the Island and its strained communication
camouflaged ships ploughing through the disastrous ocean

my father held in mid-career

The lodging house landlady spied the damage worked
into the wall by the beating of our intruding feet
just above the wainscoting as the band approached
down the street unseen and we leaned far out
and the marching soldiers were coming into view
with the drums and the bugles and the thud   thud   thud
We beat in our toe-hold till the plaster crumbled
and the wrath of the landlady came to defend it

3 Warworkers

What will pull War One forth as part of today?
Will the story of the Misses Bigg do it
how they started their ballet out of a few dance steps,
a little drawing room class, and decked their pupils in flags
and set up such a display
that it got on stage and was signalled
to all around as the Patriotic Ballet
depicting, demonstrating the right spirit for all Allies?

Rose tells another story of the proper kind
secure in her position of scullery maid
to the lodging house trade, upstairs and down
with buckets, mops, and trays
but mostly, it seemed to lodgers, kneeling in grates
setting fire to the crumpled news of yesterday's battles
soldiers dying at the front across the Channel, lighting
a twist of paper, if possible, from yesterday's coals,
placing the kindling and the new coals and the flames

Any connection was greater than any other status
What light falls on the human scene embattled?

Most sweeping of connections in power to proceed
was the Misses Bigg's Ballet   what brought them forth?
a compulsion to do their bit that got into step
Miss Bigg and her sister, Miss Bigg, designated by size

Rose came out from her place in the basement
walked the Leas and met soldiers strolling three abreast
One broke off one day   from far away

walked with her and climbed down the chalky cliff
to the shrubs below (as for chosen WAACs they did)
She wore a flower from someone's hedge when he went
  away to fight

Down to the quay at length the soldiers marched
and the camouflaged transport took them out of sight
Bands were silent during this last lap

Guns could be heard thudding in that opposite land
shown on a clear day in its cliff lines
Flags waved from the hotels still and the bands played
Ships from the quay put out and returned

One who was a child then looks back
on this small part of the scene for exact
views in bright outlines emerging and disappearing

4 Keeping Going

What kept that War going whatever the cost?
Could it have been the Misses Bigg?
This was a vast time for those two spirits
the little girls
had varying degrees of responses and their small lithe bodies
took the motion from the ponderous ones above them
War brought the Misses Bigg out of the shadows
of spinsterhood and the beginnings of decline and was a
    forward
movement with repercussions (still) to our lasting good

Could it have been the Skinners in their minor profiteering
measuring out the bread and the milk for their boarders,
children sheltered here from the earth's many corners,
fed, in the embargo, off the allotment garden,
a little going a long way at the long board table
Mr. Skinner, for Victory, eating porridge without sugar?

Could it have been Rose?

Such a contribution can't be measured

Could it have been the soldiers themselves, the most
    oppressed of them
in the long trenches dying out of the scene
or the victims of the air-raids
those great sung passed-away, recorders of only part of
    what went on
and in idea the least of it   "We are the dead sung"
each with enough action   to stop himself

or the stricken alive   dead to all else
talking out the battles till their breath is dust

Sing on, flags   and drumbeats my father heard
though gone from there and not again the same
        stir in the heart that takes the man abroad
to the War because he can't stay away
drawn by the bugle, the drum, the marching and the horses
    fleet

yet still the terrible eruptions can break on
to claim the first World War for now and now
its waves of terror travelling to the furthest shore

5 Survivors

How prove that World War One is of our time
we really can't through the dead

but through those who rose into New Being
busy in their pocket of place, Folkestone
out of that setting and the way it enhanced
with lights   bands   marching   blackouts   sirens
other stimulation of the warpath
while the sacrificed go down into the massive past

And those who kept the War as fought alive
in talk   in wounds   in medals' argument
with weeping muffled   make a background

to
Miss Bigg and her sister Miss Bigg, each to her size
Rose after the soldier she found
the Skinner couple with the boarding school for strangers
the Wartime landladies and the Invaders
the wounded promenading with the nurses' aides
(while the Resort's still prominent invalids
take the air too and listen to the waves)

the ships pulling away to cross the Channel
the searchlights and the sirens keeping the war in place

6 An End in View

By night we crouched   we hoped unseen
guarding ourselves with a sweeping beam
that lit the Channel waves and then the moon

Long   long behind are left
the machinations of potentates whose movements spread
to later concentrations
edged on like waves
long   long behind are left those dead

Some things that popped up   sometimes very bright
were the fresh flowers perhaps
an unclassed society   women untrammelled
business blossoming new canons for its rightness

the flag waving went on   the drummed marching
moved away to the quay   was lost in the ocean
of waves the Channel carried between the chalk cliffs
of Calais and Folkestone   and the land of the thudding
    guns
was another part of the tale

Moving In

Some principle of existence was discovered
as we moved into buildings   buffeted
by seasons circling such a hilltop
and all the possessions reaching out

discovered by whom?   I think my memory goes
to the right source of that: a child past twelve
waiting to depart from all the years
led around   and launch into the fields   fenced or not
and pastures with the high imbedded rocks

and down the fields the river   and up the reach
of field path and then road   the moon above
and distances known only when we got
that first of animals   the horse

and with the coming cold the barn I entered
going out by dawn to feed the bulky horses
pressing into the stall where the hoofs stamped

here on my own   chosen from unimportance
to feel the weather of a continent
upon a hill   and running down to a beach
and back into forest where a fence meandered
grey poles criss-crossed in a past diligence
recognized only by the pastured horses
as still authority over the earth

                or by myself who counted likely to stay
root-rock in pasture   orchard trees decaying
yet spread too   so the apples reappear
mottled and shrunken   seedy   tart to the core

then the eye fell on what was possible
            and stunted growth caught up   and time to come
could go back to this form of how to dwell

The Forest

One hundred acres and a stream:
this we had when we were poor
eating mostly apples, but an occasional bit more,

catching in the stream trout like sunbeams
here the great flat stones
divided the water's rush   and the great firs
stood in close to the alders
and on, on and on   travelling the miles

This we had when we were poor   and the few animals
to do our bidding lived on the lean acres
closest to the home of barn and other buildings
including the bleak house without accoutrements
built in   and the woodlands stretched and stretched
and one old horse   hauled logs in for the winter
that was long   long   and heavy with snow

This we had when we were poor,
miles that would bring now the thirsty birds
to a retreat   the bear, the moose
the person to the point of truth

And the stream running through them was a possession
none can match now, curling among the alders
dipping under the firs, parting to stones
and under the little bridge of logs
pushing its way to the clear river   miles lower, on, on

A River Story

The river helps the characters
bring their comedy to a close   the villain drowns
the logs come safe to the mill from the primal forest

The villain drowned   the boats beached   the canoe
floating upside down   and now a wedding
gives new ascendancy promise

But then the poem breathes   claims the river injured
goes on with sequels

The villain swings in weed   still unextinguished
the miles go on   the river sliding at dawn
the islands revealed

How beautiful they are   sequel on sequel
the stories unfold   diminishing as repeated
even though busier   the motor boats put forth

The islands still can catch a morning radiance
within the mist   but few wings rise to meet it
or fish to net

The villain swings   within the weed entangled
never to dissolve   they say   how dignified
his many endeavours   and the river sighs
sliding along its course
bewildered by itself   holding the stars

The poem is not the story as it was told
but trails out of it and is at loss
among the islands scented with their own plants

Development as sequel is always strange
those characters are ghosts   even the islands

From a River Boat

I saw out the open doorway of the hold
the river writing a page
line on line   this is a way to read

Here it seems that to move
through wrinkles of running water is to be all we need

The sun is not shining   the wind
is only enough to set up little waves

To be absorbed in this writing   in this silvery word
is to by-pass identity it has seemed
to be all the way composed
in a quiet meditation obliquely told

Look too at the water to see an outlook of history
a written page flowing along into fresh impulse
here charging the surface of words the silent and spoken
    records
and the wind turning the lines into another outburst

The Poets of Home

I in my age am sent
the poems of the dead
who are melted down to themselves

who lie in the thin wafers
who are holy and consumed for love

who are back in their time
who are in their native land
or journeying to return

They are over and done with
so they can return to be
the next people's splendour

I envy them their breath that is not
I envy them no tomorrow
I envy them the poem grown like a flower
that shall be picked by everyone
that passes   and the native
land of their dust

The Flight of Stars

I pray to do a poem   that captures   the stars that rush
flown light away from here   away from place
not lighting this one world   overmuch

This is the equivalent in space
to the long thought that never finds its peace

One world is left in what it claims to be place
for all its parallels and explosives

One world and what is it doing in the rush
that loses stars each incandescent night
and stays in darkness with a flight of stairs going up

I feel so strange when I think of how the years
travel their courses in us   these episodes
a must   when brought to bed we lie with ourselves
and those to be the next people   and so always

There are the golden adventures   and I lived
in envy and emulation of them
sometimes this feeling

could take far out   where at some point the vanguard
fled in full charge of the void ahead
            wherever they are   come followers of the lead

and for this star   don't know the pace   but find
a stair in some old quarter   going up

to where it vanishes   and is lost   the lights
don't pierce   the mist even   ghostly reinforce
step demarcations from an earlier age

ringing its bells in darkness of the distance

Notes on the Author

One of Canada's most anthologized female poets, Dorothy Roberts was born in Fredericton, New Brunswick, on 6 July 1906, the daughter of poet Theodore Goodridge Roberts and Frances Allen Roberts. Although she has lived most of her adult life in the United States, Roberts is firmly rooted in Canada, as is her poetry in the austere landscape of the North.

A writer whose work is marked by a firm intelligence, Roberts has drawn together for this, her seventh volume of poetry, a collection of later life poems in which she unflinchingly confronts the polarities of birth and death, the pleasures of age and the interwoven pattern of loss.

✳

"In her poetry, Dorothy Roberts observes the warm and precise exchanges that exist between the great world outdoors and our domestic interiors, between the present and the past. She traces the passage of sunlight from one window to the next, as seen by the patient inhabitant, and the movement of lamps from window to window, as seen by the passing stranger. These poems from the far corners of a life are unprecedented and unparalleled, beautiful as a ship on the horizon sailing away, sailing home."
— Emily Grosholz, Advisory Editor
for *Hudson Review*

"Nothing in our poetry remotely resembles this brilliant 'flight of stars' of Dorothy Roberts, poems written with undiminished power toward the close of a long life — a voice, in Wallace Stevens' phrase, that makes 'the sky acutest at its vanishing.' Her poems of childhood are at once intimately present and eighty years distant, lit windows where a woman's moving figure shapes the lights against the Northern dark Like the growing rings on a tree, her original syntax and images carry with authority the fullness of time's circularity and its onwardness"

— Eleanor Wilner, Editor of *Calyx* magazine